How to use this book

Follow the advice, in italics, given for you on each page.
Support the children as they read the text that is shaded in cream.
***Praise** the children at every step!*

Detailed guidance is provided in the Read Write Inc. Phonics Handbook

9 reading activities

Children:

Practise reading the speed sounds.

Read the green, red and challenge words for the story.

Listen as you read the introduction.

Discuss the vocabulary check with you.

Read the story.

Re-read the story and discuss the 'questions to talk about'.

Read the story with fluency and expression.

Answer the questions to 'read and answer'.

Practise reading the speed words.

LITTLE EALING
SCHOOL
W5 4EA
020 8567 2135

Speed sounds

Consonants *Say the pure sounds (do not add 'uh').*

f	l	m	n	r	s	v	z	sh	th	ng
ff	ll	mm	nn	rr	ss	ve	zz			nk
			kn				s			

b	c	d	g	h	j	p	qu	t	w	x	y	ch
bb	k	dd	gg			pp		tt	wh			**tch**
	ck											

Vowels *Say the sounds in and out of order.*

at	hen	in	on	up	day	see	high	blow
	head					happy	find	no

zoo	look	car	for	fair	whirl	shout	boy
			door				spoil
			snore				

*Each box contains one sound but sometimes more than one grapheme. Focus graphemes are **circled**.*

Green words

Read in Fred Talk (pure sounds).

three way high lay batch

know grow own sow bowl

Read in syllables.

rad\`ish	→	radish	pack\`et	→	packet
fan\`tas\`tic	→	fantastic	sa\`lad	→	salad
a\`way	→	away	shall\`ow	→	shallow
win\`dow	→	window	com\`post	→	compost
na\`rrow	→	narrow	spa\`rrow	→	sparrow

Read the root word first and then with the ending.

seed	→	seeds	week	→	weeks
row	→	rows	slow	→	slowly
grow	→	grown			

Red words

their you your want some they

are small of the fall call any fall*

Challenge words

every wash length

*Red word for this story only

Grow your own radishes

Introduction

What is the difference between a fiction book and a non-fiction book? This book tells us how to grow radishes. There are very clear instructions.

Find out what you need, what to do and how long it takes.

Story written by Gill Munton
Illustrated by Tim Archbold

Vocabulary check

Discuss the meaning (as used in the story) after the children have read each word.

	definition:	sentence/phrase:
crop	*lot or load*	*You can grow your very own crop of radishes.*
sow	*plant seeds in the earth*	*If you want lots, sow a batch of seeds every three weeks.*
shallow	*not deep*	*a shallow plant pot or window box*
compost	*loose soil*	*a bag of potting compost*
level	*top*	*The seeds must be below the level of the compost.*
damp	*slightly wet*	*Keep the compost damp, ...*
weeds	*plants you don't want*	*and pull out any weeds.*

Punctuation to note in this story:

1. *Capital letters to start sentences and full stops to end sentences*
2. *Capital letters for names*
3. *Exclamation marks to show anger, shock and surprise*
4. *'Wait and see' dots...*

Grow your own radishes

Did you know that you can grow
your very own crop of radishes
in just three weeks?

You must sow the seeds in the spring.
If you want lots of fresh radishes,
sow a batch of seeds every three weeks.

Let me show you the best way to grow your own radishes!

You will need:

- a packet of radish seeds
- a shallow plant pot or a window box
- a bag of potting compost
- some sand
- a black bin bag

What to do:

1. Fill the plant pot or window box with potting compost.

2. Lay some sand on top of the compost.

3. Sow the seeds in three rows.
The seeds must be just below the
level of the compost.

4. Put a sheet of black bin bag on the top.
This will help the seeds to grow,
as well as stopping sparrows from
pecking them up.

5. Ask a grown-up to help you to put the pot or window box outside in a sunny spot on a window sill, away from the wind. (If the window sill is very narrow, the pot may fall off.)

6. The radish plants will slowly begin to grow. (The small plants are called seedlings.) Then you can lift off the bin bag.

7. Keep the compost damp, and pull out any weeds that grow in the pot or window box.

8. Keep checking the radish plants.
When they are 10cm high,
radishes will have grown below the compost.

9. (This is the best bit!) Pull up the radishes when they are 2-3cm long.
(You can check their length if you push back a bit of compost.)

10. Mix up a fantastic fresh radish salad! Wash the radishes well, and put them in a big bowl.

    Then you can add chopped carrots, leeks, cress, shallots, or nuts.

Questions to talk about

Re-read the page. Read the question to the children. Tell them whether it is a **FIND IT** *question or* **PROVE IT** *question.*

FIND IT

- ✓ *Turn to the page*
- ✓ *Read the question*
- ✓ *Find the answer*

PROVE IT

- ✓ *Turn to the page*
- ✓ *Read the question*
- ✓ *Find your evidence*
- ✓ *Explain why*

Page 9:	FIND IT	*How long does it take to grow radishes?*
Page 10:	PROVE IT	*Why are there five bullet points on this page?* *(Check that the children know what a bullet point is.)*
Page 11:	FIND IT	*What must you do after putting compost in the pot?*
Page 12:	FIND IT	*Why must you put a bin bag on the top of the pot?*
Page 13:	FIND IT	*When do you take the bin bag off?*
Page 14:	PROVE IT	*How do you know when the radishes have grown below the soil?*
Page 15:	PROVE IT	*How could you eat the radishes?*

Questions to read and answer

(Children complete without your help.)

1. You can grow your own radishes in **six weeks / one week / three weeks.**

2. You need to fill the plant pot with **sand / potting compost / bin bags.**

3. The plant pot must be in **a dark spot / a sunny spot / the wind.**

4. Radishes will have grown below the compost when the plants are **25cm high / 5cm high / 10cm high.**

5. You can add the radishes to **a salad / the compost.**

Speed words

Children practise reading the words across the rows, down the columns and in and out of order clearly and quickly.

three	high	fall	stopping	sunny
seeds	window	own	below	slowly
grow	bowl	pull	push	put
they	are	weed	you	your